T0083517

The Last Visit

The Last Visit

poems

Chad Abushanab

AUTUMN
HOUSE PRESS
pittsburgh

 Autumn House Press receives state arts funding support through a grant from the Pennsylvania Council on the Art, a state agency funded by the Commonwealth of Pennsylvania, and the National Endowment for the Arts, a federal agency.

Cover art: Angus Macpherson, "The Lamp," 12" x 12", giclée print. Albuquerque painter represented at Sumner & Dene Gallery, www.sumnerdene.com.

Text and cover design: Chiquita Babb

ISBN: 978-1-938769-37-5
Library of Congress Control Number: 2018952005

For my mother

Contents

Negatives under Microscope

I'm focused on the space inside your eyes—
first pupil, then iris, now cellular disruption—
in search of some clear catalyst, some reason
for these scars, for this crooked helix on my chest.
I want the DNA for empty bottles.
I need to know what made your cruelties grow
unwieldy, like cancers let loose upon a body.
I've scoured the entire frame, pushed past
the edge of every family negative
believing the secret's hidden, like a code
between the plastic and the acetate.
I stare for hours at a single portrait,
deducing from a smile the hell behind your face.
At times I think I smell the whisky sweet
perfume of you, as though each image captured
something of how you lived, how you breathed.
But then each clue turns out a part of me:
a hair, a thumbprint left while leafing through
the pile of specimens, a flake of skin,
a barely visible scratch I made in haste—
more me than you, more you than science,
naked and pinned down beneath the lens,
as though our cause is finally in the frame,
begging for exposure, for the light.

The Factory

Hulks in shadows just outside of town:
a rusted mess, a postindustrial tomb.
Poorwills roost in smokestacks falling down
and cry out something awful in the gloom.

Elsewhere, men with bloody lungs keep
coughing up clots like overripe berries.
Their wives beside them pretend to be asleep,
imagine different endings to their stories.

Plastic Men

After each fight, Mom took us both
to Wilson's Five & Dime to pick
some cheap toys. Our father's slurred voice
became a ghost of breath beneath
the long tin ventilation shafts.
Mom waited by the counter,
spoke to the clerk about discontinued
spools of thread, buttons she'd meant
to sew on weeks ago. She wore
green bruises below her eyes.
Her split lip kept her dabbing blood
with Kleenex—a poppy flowered rag.
Digging through crates of army men,
we looked for figures of tragedy:
missing arms, hands broken at the wrist,
the grenadier who'd gripped the bomb
too long. Back home, we'd line up the men
on our bedroom windowsill. We smiled
at our army of maimed green soldiers.
They could not raise their voices despite
their mortal wounds, their missing limbs.

The Way

The day I found him doesn't stand apart
from any other, save for how a rain
cooled the afternoon and left the hills
smelling of steam and creeping amber rosin.
The afternoons were hot, and beneath the shade
of spruce and pine I followed narrow creeks
until their quiet, strangled ends. I searched

for caves and the remains of ancient arrowheads.
The woods were deep and took me far from home.
Failing light made shapes look soft, unclear,
and at first it seemed he might be drunk or sleeping—
he slouched against a sweetgum tree, and maybe,
I thought, I saw him move, or twitch, or flinch.
The sudden stench of rot said otherwise.

His eyes were open, clouded over, blank
much like the sky now hidden by the trees.
He sat surrounded by fallen ochre leaves,
legs splayed out into wide, facing angles.
A film of something green touched his lips,
swollen from the heavy August heat.
He gripped a small revolver in his hand.

Behind his head: the splintered trunk, a ring
of blackened blood, glittering fragments of bone.
I froze, afraid the slightest move might bring
him back, might wake him from his bleeding slumber.
I watched until the red sun died away,
and darkness dimmed that shining in his eyes.
It seemed this scene had been set up for me.

He walked into the woods to die, while the sun
drew out the long shadows of the forest.
And when the gun went off, there was no shudder
among the trees, no importance felt
by the birds, just violence and the body, waiting
for me, the pupil, who wanders in the woods,
already on a path toward knowing death.

Dead Town

A dead town full of ghosts—it left behind
its brick and mortar bones, the pharmacy
windows dark with dust. Each day we find
the Bijoux Movie House's bleached marquee
unchanged, and no one really seems to mind.
7:00—*The Day The Earth Stood Still*.
The seats stay empty since they closed the mill.

Instead, we haunt the Late-Nite A & P,
the last place left to shop for Wonder Bread,
Del Monte peaches, and Chef Boyardee.
We eat our dinners sitting up in bed.
For company, the rabbit-eared TV.
Infomercials fill the anxious quiet,
the midnight mantra, "Don't believe us? Try it!"

echoes through our rooms paid by the week.
It drowns the sound of industry collapsing,
the deafening crash of silence at its peak—
no cars, no crowds, the old mill making nothing—
the sound of losing purpose, so to speak.
Our part-time days, like stories stretched too thin,
cannot escape the were, and was, and when.

Ghazal

When my father left for good, we were living in the desert.
I wouldn't cry for him. My eyes became a desert.

Toward Your Understanding

You believe your father is made of stone,
a tower whose strength is silence.
Neither of you speak. This is not unusual.
Today he walks ahead, leads you
down Cranberry Lane, to White Horse,
where you are outside the dead man's house.

Your father says, "He shot himself in there,"
a white house with a browning lawn
and a single twisted-up crepe myrtle.
And maybe because it looks so familiar—
like your own home—this does not frighten you.
Your father says, "He shot himself in the head."

He leads you to the window, grips your waist
and lifts you to the darkened glass.
Your reflection fades into the room,
sparsely furnished, gray carpet, white walls.
You see it there above the sofa: a blossom
of blood, a ring fanning out to nothing.

In the center of the plaster: a small black hole.
It seems, somehow, impossibly empty.
When you're lowered back to the ground,
you feel the neighborhood beneath your feet.
Even the bone-white sun is fading faster
than it should. You know it will be dark soon.

Missing

When Bea McConnell disappeared,
she was only eight years old,
and because of what our parents feared
the neighborhood went cold.

We saw the posters everywhere,
the broken nose, the curls.
The frightened words above her hair
said *Have You Seen This Girl?*

We started locking doors at night
though we never did before.
No matter the hour, we burned the light
that hung above our door.

Police put corpse-dogs on the trail
and dragged the quarry lake.
They looked in every open well
in hopes the case would break.

It never did. The posters faded.
In time, so did the search.
Her parents, pale as plaster, waited.
They often cried in church.

Like the nights I'd hear my mother weep
and open my bedroom door,
and I'd pretend I was asleep
as she slowly crossed the floor.

She'd place her hand upon my head,
her fingers light as air,
and whisper in a voice like lead
a single, shaken prayer:

"Dear God, please let my child stay.
I know that you are just.
I need him to survive the day.
Take others if you must."

Confession: Silva's Quarry

"It seemed we were doing some good
by dumping the body in the quarry;
that each ballast we stuffed down her throat
to pull her toward the bottom
was a good intention approaching salvation
not for ourselves but for others, say,
her family, or friends, who might be haunted
by the sight of her for lifetimes to follow.
We brushed her nails clean and never
undressed her. We wrapped her in a sheet.
When Vaughn rolled her down the hill toward
the mossy rocks, with Sid out in front,
walking backwards, stepping over roots
to control her descent, her arm lolled out,
got spotted with leaves, and we stopped
to wrap her up again. We picked debris
from her forearms, hair, thighs, and wrists.
It was a wasted effort, we all knew that,
and so no one had to say it as we stood
by the quarry's edge. Out on the black water
a small snake swam, made ripples
as it approached our shadows, which were long.
The water lapped at the granite, and an owl,
or something, moved beyond the branches of a tree,
prompting me to stand. I'm the one who nudged her
over the edge, and we watched as she sank,
the water bubbled, and her shadow disappeared
as though ink had spread about the pool."

Boys

The fall of '93. Red leaves
drift, spinning toward the ground,
and pile beneath the schoolyard eaves.
Once struck, he just stays down,

swallows back his shock and tears.
It's me who picked the fight,
and I'll carry on this way for years.
I pack a solid right

left bloodied by his broken lips.
I lift my arms to play
the victor, satisfy the script.
But before I walk away,

back home where my dad swills gin,
curses game-show hosts,
and trucks of smuggled Mexicans,
I know I've made the most

of fear. Today I am a man.
My dad will sure be proud.
The rest, stunned silent when this began,
are cheering, wild and loud.

Found Dead in the Sequatchie Valley

They found her body lying here
    between the skeletons of pine.
        Like by some design
    she died in fall, the time of year

when shadows kissed her thin wrists,
    and the sun, at last, turned cold and white,
        a ball of frozen light.
    The talk is vague, but most insist

her boyfriend led her to the hollow
    at night, they had a fight, she
        was newly pregnant, and he
    was mad, and madness is what followed.

The stories try to get at reason,
    but the local papers let it go,
        leaving these woods to know
    or to forget. Now's the season

when the dead wind mimics the desperate cries,
    the purple clover turns to brown,
        and all the lights in town
    look far away, like listless eyes.

And I wonder what's out here to learn
    besides the silence of these hills
        once final sunlight fills
    the valley like a broken urn?

It cannot hold. The light escapes
　　as though it's liquid through a sieve,
　　　　and I want to believe—
　　as all gets tangled in the drapes

of night—in wholeness, if not peace.
　　The girl is dead. Her voice is lost
　　　　in all the stories tossed
　　like leaves when autumn strips the trees.

What happened here, we'll never know.
　　These secrets make the kudzu grow.

The Dive

A busted exit sign above the door
invites no one to leave. The windows are barred,
and the panes themselves are painted over with tar.
No question as to what this place is for.

The regulars all stare into their drinks,
lamenting futures, forgetting pasts. Bar stools
are split at every seam. The Tavern Rules
say *No Cussing*, though mostly no one speaks.

They're married to their grief, you think. But here
you are: Jack Daniel's and your worries. The same
as any drunk who will not lay the blame
on himself, drowning instead in whisky and beer.

A man with roadmap eyes searches his pockets
for jukebox change and comes up short. Instead,
the ceiling fan keeps rhythm while each dead
minute tumbles off the Highlife clock. "It's

closing time!" Time for another drink.
The barkeep brings it over, snatches the cash,
flicks his cigarette and drops the ash
into the rusted pit of a clogged-up sink.

This dive, this glass, these greasy fingerprints,
they're each a part of something very old:
a need to slow the way a story's told
to keep it all from making too much sense.

The Future of the Past

We thought we would, by now, retire the wheel;
that we could lay to rest that early invention.
Instead, the sidewalks just became more cracked,
more broken apart by wild vegetation
pushing through fissures in worn-out roads.
The movies lied. They promised us new modes
of transportation, but science fiction lacked
the science frame by frame and reel by reel.

Our stories rarely end in slow dissolve,
a fleur of music, credits, special thanks
to all of those that made this possible.
There are no squibs, no CGI, no blanks.
Our futures stall, our cars will never fly,
and when our loves begin to die, they die.
We always want what's most improbable.
Our hearts, like the first machines, do not evolve.

To Speak of Woe That Is in Marriage

When his drinking gets bad, she cannot meet his eye.
He stays out late. Out where? She does not know.
He sweats Manhattans, answers slurred and slow,
and staggers while he's conjuring a lie.

She hides his keys—the wreck not long ago—
then holds him shaking in the upstairs hall
as he talks her into "one more drink, that's all."
The years of bargains wore her down, and so

tonight she listens for his breath to fall
into a raspy sleep. When the powder glow
of not-quite-dawn falls on her naked woe,
she writes a note (*I've gone—PLEASE DO NOT CALL*)

then tears it up, resigned to quantify
the endless nights it takes for him to die.

Cheating in a Small Town

It was dim enough to call it dark,
an amber bulb the only light.
The Jameson had done its work
to complicate the wrong and right.
Her wedding photo on the shelf
looked down on us. We didn't quit.
We got undressed in spite of it,
as though we couldn't stop ourselves.

I wanted this. I wanted to know
the harm we'd cause, the damage done
by giving in, by letting go.
I knew her daughter slept just down
the hall, her husband was on a job
in Memphis. I had so much less
to lose, my life already a mess.
After, when she began to sob,

I left. The light was creeping in
to expose our nakedness, our sin.
On my way out the door, I said
that I'd come back. I never did.

Ghazal

We packed our clothes in garbage bags, rented filthy rooms.
How many cheap motels line the highways of the desert?

Again

She's bleeding from the mouth again.
Each drop that slips between her fingers,
spatters the countertop, and blooms
like tiny poppies on the tile.
He's split her lip with the backhand
I've feared as long as I can remember.
But she is not afraid. My mother
provokes him. Spits his name like poison.
She smiles wide, the words swelling
to cancer, toxic, eating her guts.

Tomorrow, she'll drive miles out
of town to shop where no one knows
her face. She'll laugh when the pretty cashier
asks if she got into a fight,
when loading up the car she'll save
the frozen peas to press against
the cut that weeps beneath her cheek.

Layover after Visiting My Father

A woman dressed in black pajamas
waiting to fly to Houston grips
her cell phone like a bludgeon,

speaks in silent wisps of teeth
and tongue, and stumbles when she shuts
her eyes. She's telling him, the one

who isn't worth forgiveness,
he is forgiven once again.
She's holding back what's left of love.

When we meet eyes across the gate,
I know what keeps her up at night
like splintered ribs that will not mend.

Poem Begun in a West Texas Corn Maze

I listen for children shouting through the dried-
up stalks, but all I hear are whispers and crows,
what few remain. For over an hour I've tried
to solve the maze, navigate its rows,

and now the comforting smell of funnel cake
has faded. In the crisp, October cold,
the families have started home; their brake
lights burn beyond the field. I shiver and fold

my arms. A cool, translucent moon rises,
and I quicken my pace to reach some final gate.
Is it left? Or right? The sudden dark disguises
the way, and I half-remember another late

autumn, when I was nine and playing here.
The sun fell soft behind the stalks and I ran
further into the dark while closing time grew near.
I recall it still, but no longer understand

the thrill of bolting, blind and breathless, deep
into the maze. I know those days have run
their course, since now I cannot help but keep
the end in mind, the setting of the sun,

the fallen ears of corn gone soft and rotten.
It works against these paths and how they're crossed
to spark in us, again, the long forgotten
joy of the deliberately lost.

Ghazal

I wrote him a letter once but left it in a motel drawer.
To where could I address it? The envelope said *Desert*.

A Haunted House

Just like me, it fell apart:
the doorway left a toothless mouth
that couldn't hold back its history.

More rotten, less recognizable
each day. Strangled by weeds until
it looked more like kudzu vine than house.

The paint gone sick and flaking off.
The garden rushed by wild grass,
until the fall, when everything dies,

except the henbits and dead nettles.
They sprout with superstitions, and spread
about the same: everywhere.

Leaving town tonight, I see it
parched like a skull just off the road.
Ten years ago, I made love

among its graveyard of empty cans,
the moonlight shining through the holes
punched in the rusted-out tin roof.

I remember mice and rotten cloth,
the feeling of October's fingers
sliding along our nakedness;

being stripped of all my flesh,
a pile of bones that couldn't be a body
despite what she was whispering.

Restless

What comes, then, of the man who crept
into his study late at night
and typed by dull green banker's light
while others slept?

His wife would toss and turn in bed,
and lay her arm across his chest.
He loved her but he couldn't rest.
He wrote instead

some lines about his childhood,
a girl whose hand he used to grip.
He wished he could kiss her bottom lip
but never would.

The loves that sleep inside the mind
are steeped in restless mystery.
Not bound by time or history,
they rather find

a quiet nook to turn and toss
and wake a husband in the dark—
a warm and wanton question mark
to hang his loss.

Custody Denied

The subject, *A*, is hereby deemed unfit
to care for his two sons, *B* and *C*.
His love, no matter how they want for it,

is problematic. Subject says he quit
abusing alcohol, but smelled of whisky.
The subject, *A*, is hereby deemed unfit

for visitation rights, unless observed and split
between locations found clean and hazard-free.
His love, even though they want for it,

cannot excuse his sudden, violent fits.
I recommend a psych exam. See:
when subject was told he's hereby deemed unfit,

he threatened to beat the social worker, hit
the table with his fists. She agrees
his love is toxic. Still, they want for it.

The boys will be removed, pending this writ,
and cared for by the state of Tennessee.
The father, *A*, is hereby deemed unfit
to love, no matter how they want for it.

Ghazal

When I drink my head fills up with sand.
I cut myself but do not bleed. I'm empty as a desert.

Roadkill Ode

I find you broken—
a mottled possum dead beside the road,
mouth regal, painted red,
teeth still sharp and proud.

Your eye protrudes miraculously
from the weeping socket,
looks back on a life made fat
by what was discarded.

How many empty cans of beans
turned into your goblets,
adorned with rust, collecting
a thick sweet drink of rain?

At night you shook the brush,
guided by the scent of rotten apple cores.
The flies respected your desires
and kept their distance while you ate.

You were king and court.
Your reign was one of tousled dust
and dark, a headlong plunge
toward betrayal by two headlights and a tire.

Did the crack of your spine
strike you as undignified?
From the way your nose points to the curb
it looks like you almost made it back.

Or were you crawling, inching
to the fallen leaves,
to dig yourself a grave?
Oh, I know that I'm not whole,

and sometimes feel the flies swarming,
like much of me is rotten.

Visiting My Own Grave

The plot next door has complex etchings, flowers,
crawling vines that intertwine like figures
on an ancient urn, while mine is squat and square:
a simple granite marker, my name, the dates.
It feels like something brought me here, but I,
not knowing what to do, just steal some flowers
from the nicer, neighboring plot to praise my memory
(my thanks to Daniel Johns, d. 1990).
I say a dead prayer. For whom? I'm not quite sure.
I'm not—or wasn't—a man who went to church.
I never believed in the way believers do.
But here I am the same, though shadow, though shade.
I stand unseen, unheard, above the spot
where my body rots in a very plain box.
When I came back, I wandered the earth for a while.
My spirit did, I should say. And when I say
"the earth," I really mean my neighborhood.
You know—the street I lived on, the grocery store.
I walked the aisles touching things I bought
back then and noticed how the bright clear light
of hanging halogens made each tomato
burst with a red more vibrant than anything
I'd seen before—back when I was alive.
That's the only beauty when you're dead:
the things you knew, ignored, and now have lost.
Tomatoes, bottles gleaming in piles of garbage,
the shades of pearl in a pool of motor oil.
The wind picks up and cuts between the graves.
A figure stands a hundred yards away
framed in the dark between two concrete angels.
There is no moon, no stars. It's impossible
to tell a mourner from a ghost—

Halloween

For Halloween this year I'll be a man.
I'll work my hands to bloody rags and use
my fists to prove which truths I understand.

I'll paint my face into a mask of bruise
like coming home after a barroom fight.
A man should fight, my father said, and lose

sometimes—no matter if he's wrong or right.
I'll swallow up a pint of Cutty Sark.
I'll stumble home and fumble with the light.

He said if you drink, you won't feel the marks,
you'll never know the places where you've bled.
For Halloween, I drink the autumn dark.

I'll be a man the way my father said.
On Halloween, we're closer to the dead.
His teeth were crooked. His hands were red.

Love Poem with Five Lines Stolen from VHS Boxes

My clothes became too tight, and crescent claws
broke through my fingertips. "It's beautiful,"
you said, while floating down the spiral stairs.
I wallowed in your want for me and tore
your powder evening gown to ribbons. You fit
me with a studded leash, a mongrel beast
who writhed beside your feet and lapped the pools
of moonlight from the street. I loved the way
you made me less than a man. I loved the way
you fed me from your hand and told me good
when I was being bad. I drank the blood
of alley cats I snared between my teeth.
From what I can recall, the lust for meat
was terrible and sweet. I swallowed all I could,
then you sent me out for more. When neighbor kids
began to disappear, you stroked my head.
You watched old horror tapes for strategies
to keep me wild, hidden, yours. For weeks,
I stayed inside. I fed on bones and rot.
You sat in the window and wished away the sun.
You asked of me just who is more depraved,
the monster or the one who made him so?
Your love's like blood. It coats my hungry tongue.
For reasons such as these, I still don't know.

Drive-In

Footsteps stop outside the door.
His heavy boots divide the light
that creeps across her bedroom floor,
and the knob turns slowly to the right.

Forever, she'll replay this scene.
The killer grins down from the screen.
Inside a desperate, foggy car,
her pleated skirt is pushed too far.

Ghazal

Ten years later: I step barefoot on broken glass.
I search for leftover Jack like water in the desert.

Drinking All Night in Tennessee

The night is long, and whisky kills the minutes.
It makes the hour cry. There's nothing in it.

But you're too drunk to listen. It's the sound
a hostage makes when hope of being found

is lost. He sees the end, knows he will die
as sure as there is blackness in the sky.

It's the sound you make when everyone's asleep
and the sun has yet to ribbon on the steep

array of mountains just beyond the hills.
You have your coffee cup of Jack, your pills.

And, because you can't take one more second
of slow, deliberate suicide, you reckon

to scream but only sigh, and pop the top
from off the plastic amber bottle, then stop.

The sun, at last, has crested on the ridge,
its crooked spine on fire like a page

that's torn and burned for what it might reveal.
Soon, the sun will light the room. You'll heal,

and sleep, and steel yourself to have the wounds
torn open again, forever, until you've found

an antidote for grief, a lasting relief,
something stronger than liquor, like belief.

Small Funeral

I find him curled up on the lawn,
a silver tom turned stiff with frost.
A portion of his skull is gone.
A frozen ring of blood's been tossed

in jagged splashes. Now here he lies,
where first November ice preserves
the violence for my morning eyes.
Its monument goes undisturbed.

I think about my brother, dead
at twenty, the broken window glass,
the stench of burning flesh, his head
cracked open in the moonlit grass,

and I know a tombstone is less real
than records of post-mortem harms.
Or bodies twisted up in steel.
Or bones that sprout from broken arms.

Some are left as misshapen vessels
mangled beyond the point of prayer
when morning mist dissolves like angels
and night escapes the fuel-soaked air.

I kneel beside the cat and tear
his body from the greedy earth.
The ground is hard this time of year.
I'll dig a grave for what it's worth.

Desert Elegy

Mike Schiffler said, "I'm banking on the end,"
this winter while we occupied the long
oak bar at Seely's Tavern, raising defenses

one bourbon at a time. He died that May,
after the dirty piles of snow had melted
away for good. We all went to his house,

paid our respects over finger sandwiches,
the clinking of ice in tumblers like a chorus
of angels for one who dies with his hand on the bottle.

Tonight I walk out past the edge of town,
the place where streetlights barely nudge the shadows
falling from the mountain. I need a drink, and here,

this rancher's road just off of 61,
allows a man to swallow up his darkness,
disappearing—for a moment—from the world.

I drink to giving in. I drink to Mike
and to the stars, which comfort in their coldness.
A pickup crests the ridge where road meets sky.

A Voice from the Wreck

I'm an accident on the south side of the town,
>   on the outskirts, where the desert holds its ground
against the streetlights' last defenses. I'm the fire
>   leaping from the Chevy's frame to smite the sky
and drain the cool out of the night. I'm the cell phone
>   in someone's shaking hand, woken up
by the explosion in the street, the calls for help.
>   I'm an ambulance, a siren in the dark.
I'm the stoplight. I'm the kid out driving drunk,
>   vodka on his breath and bile in his throat.
I'm the headlights slamming final recognition.
>   And when you whisper names like curses
in your room, I'm the smell of gasoline in bloom,
>   the bloodstained moon behind the clouds.
I guzzle broken bones and busted radiators,
>   coolant running thick in thirsty gutters.
And if you ever manage to shut your eyes, to sleep,
>   I'll wander from the wreckage as you dream.

Ghazal

My father's voice like wind on dunes—I hear it from the bottle.
"Remember who you are," it says. "You'll never leave this desert."

Rubáiyát for My Father

This is how the cycle starts.
It binds together both our hearts
and leaves the tender skin of my back
a document of jagged marks.

I'm beaten first, then made to strip
and show you where I've met the whip.
You sterilize the harm you've done
like steady handed craftmanship.

But after the swabs and alcohol,
it's like you've never seen, at all,
the fresh wounds on my shoulder blades
or all these bloody cotton balls.

The scars get tangled on my skin
despite the cool of lanolin.
You say you love me, yes, you do,
but love has worn me ribbon-thin.

You are my father, but you are a fiend—
the one who cut and the one who cleaned,
who turned that taste of suffering
into a casual routine.

Forgive me now. This ghost I hold
is often angry, often cold,
and longs to rip the stitches out
before the wounds can go untold.

Necessary Rituals

Dip the pistol's rim in water
taking care to treat
the barrel like a damaged lover's
lacerated heart.

You should be firm but understanding.
Guide its wet snub nose
into the dish of salt, listening—
a crunch like bits of glass,

when steel is pressed into the grains,
cracks in the quiet kitchen.
This is your cue to think of Jean,
your kids, and how you miss them,

and how they walked away, left
the house a vigil
of silence. Next, you lift
the pistol by its handle,

taking a moment to gaze into
its black and absolute
mouth, knowing you were sure not to
load it with any bullets

this time—this is the ritual
and not the act.
Lower the oil-slick barrel
into your mouth and taste

the salt, and think of all that's salt.
Your once-wife's tears, the martinis
you consume without
limit. The salty largeness

of the sea, where Jean might be,
hiding away with your sons—
Stop. The next steps must be taken.
The salt will stand

static until tomorrow night's
ritual. Now set the gun
down. As you rise to turn the lights
out, dip your finger in

the bowl of ink. Make a mark
on the white refrigerator.
A family of tallies, dark
and dripping toward the floor.

Thirty-five nights. A season changed—
summer to fall—the lawns
graying, and autumn wreathes
mark every door in the neighborhood

but yours.
              When the house is dark, sleep.
Fall through the inky milk
of dreams. Think of hours
passing swiftly waiting for night.

                    You will not drink.

Repeat:

        You will not drink.

The Landlocked Lighthouse

I see its signal swing above the trees,
while driving through a storm in Tennessee.
It slices sideways, turning in the night,
and lends to someone, somewhere sense of sight.
Where does it lead? I doubt I'll ever know.
But I suspect it's where some people go.
I would not follow if I knew the source.
I've marked my map and shouldn't change my course.
Though, I'll admit I find a certain charm
in parking the car and putting on my warm
blue coat, then drifting off into the green,
like a fisherman for fish he's never seen—
who finds himself adrift, alone; his chart
wet from the rain, the only thing apart
from all the dark: the swinging of a lamp.
Though here there is no sea, just leaves and damp
soil, musky, smelling of mushrooms and mold,
like something living, fresh, but very old.
And out there, calling, is the tower's swinging
light, calling clearly as a siren's singing.
I'd like to climb those tightly spiraled stairs
and find the one who tends to the affairs
of wanderers turned searchers in the dark,
present my map, and have him make the mark.

Love Poem with Desert and Stars

We are discovering new constellations,
naming, re-naming, the shape of the stars.

Sitting by firelight, watching the clouds drift—
wraiths on the breath of a long Texas night.

This one's the Boy Who Jumped over the Nebula.
See where the seat of his pants are on fire?

Here is the Snickers Bar (south of the Milky Way)
melting as though it were left in the sun.

Shadows stretched over an ocean of desert
flicker with every lick of the wind.

Hungry and cool, coyotes are howling
filling the air with immutable song.

What if our love were as lasting as star shine,
rather than coals on a lone desert fire?

Somewhere between this blue smoke of the sky
loves such as ours get born and die.

On the Dred Ranch Road Just Off 283

Stars are fired up like scattershot.
The howls of wolves that saunter near extinction
echo across the plains until they're not.
All of them are headed one direction.

My father was a drinker. So am I—
an echo of a tune in drunken time.
The bottle is an instrument, and rye
the amber music spilling over. I'm

thinking about the rhythm of decline:
he measured his in knuckles, hookers, drinks.
I start to wonder how I'll measure mine,
the ballad of the triple-whisky jinx,

but the wind begins to sigh of tired things.
I pull the bottle from the bag. It sings.

Hometown Knowledge

And back home, someone else has killed herself—
dropped her kids at school, then killed herself.
She took her husband's war gun off the shelf

but put it back. Upstairs, she had some pills
(*It'll probably be cleaner with the pills*).
She smiled at how they used to soothe her ills,

and swallowed down a handful with apple juice.
She finished off the glass (*I forgot to buy juice*)
then ran a bath. Her limbs already loose,

she crept out of her clothes like shedding skin
(*it feels so nice to shed this heavy skin*)
and let the steaming water pull her in.

She settled against the marble, into sleep—
that's the word they always say, "sleep,"
as if one word manages to keep

the panicked, thrashing body calm and still,
the sputtering and choking calm and still,
as if it happened, somehow, beyond her will.

The whispers claim she was bound to go that way.
Her daddy and little brother went that way.
She probably waited on the day.

That's the way the stories tend to go—
They catch up with you everywhere you go.
Though you've escaped, you cannot help but know.

The Phone

There are things you can't learn over the phone,
like how each day your mother's losing weight.
Her hug has turned to a burlap sack of bones.
You imagine it sharp and cold. Her heart beats

jaggedly. There's dark beneath her eyes.
You know she cooks herself three meals a day,
but over the phone you cannot see what lies
behind her silence: she throws the food away.

She yawns and says she is a little tired,
while exhaustion settles ashen on her face.
You can't see how the neatness you admired—
the dishes clean, everything in its place—

has disappeared. The kitchen's out of order.
She doesn't make her bed. Her clothes smell bad.
And you keep moving further, moving forward
(after Dad left, you thought she'd drive you mad):

first Tennessee, then Arkansas, now Texas.
She's back home in the Carolina foothills
while the tumor near her cardiac plexus
grows. You can't see her refuse the pills,

but you hear it in each hesitation, in every
sick quiet hanging on the line.
So when she says she's "feeling better, very,"
it sends the worry ringing up your spine.

After the dial tone dies away,
you stand in the sunlight of your own kitchen.
You know she's dying, that she'll never say.
You know you will never be forgiven.

The Last Visit

I see his face as through a frosted glass,
or tears—a smearing of his present self.
I shut my eyes and wait for it to pass.

It does. These days I'm drinking less by half,
but he's stopped taking water with his rye.
He asks for something stiff from the shelf

and I begrudgingly oblige. His eyes
are red like Southern skies on August nights,
and Mother says he's started his goodbyes.

He slouches on the couch, then says outright:
"The world has gone as flat as day old beers.
So how about we drink instead of fight?"

"As father and son?" I hurl those words like spears,
and if they break the skin, he shows no pain.
"As men," he says. Then the whisky disappears.

About the Donald Justice Poetry Prize:

Made possible through the generosity of the Iris N. Spencer Poetry Award and The Spencer Family, the Donald Justice Prize honors one of our finest poets of the twentieth century. A recipient of the Pulitzer Prize, Bollingen Prize, and numerous honors for his verse, Justice was a masterful and exacting craftsman, exhibiting traits that define the prize named in his honor. The Justice Award welcomes unpublished, original book-length collections of poems that honor, create, and further the on-going pleasure and grace of form and versification. The winner of the competition will receive $1,500 and have their manuscript published.

Acknowledgments

Many thanks to the editors of the publications in which the following poems, sometimes in slightly different versions, first appeared:

32 Poems, "Halloween"

The Believer, "Silva's Quarry"

Best New Poets, "On the Dred Ranch Road Just Off 283"

Birmingham Poetry Review, "Poem Begun in a West Texas Corn Maze"

Ecotone, "Boys"

The Hopkins Review, "Dead Town," "Cheating in a Small Town," "Drinking All Night in Tennessee," and "Plastic Men"

Literary Matters, "The Dive" and "Missing"

Measure: A Review of Formal Poetry, "Girl Found Dead in the Sequatchie Valley"

The New Criterion, "Visiting My Own Grave"

The Raintown Review, "Restless"

Rockhurst Review, "Toward Your Understanding"

Shenandoah, "Small Funeral"

The Southeast Review, "The Future of the Past"

Southern Poetry Review, "A Voice from the Wreck"

The Stirring, "Love Poem with Five Lines Stolen from VHS Tapes"

Unsplendid, "Necessary Rituals"

Wildness, "Negatives under Microscope"

Thank You

I'd like to first thank my teachers: William Evans, Paul Allen, Carol Ann Davis, Mark Jarman, Kate Daniels, Rick Hillis, John Poch, William Wenthe, and Curtis Bauer. You opened worlds for me.

Thank you to Jesse Waters and everyone at the West Chester University Poetry Conference, particularly the family of Iris M. Spencer who endow the Donald Justice Poetry Prize.

A very special thank you to Jericho Brown, who not only selected this book for the Justice Prize, but was also lent his superb ear for poetry while I revised the manuscript for publication.

Thank you to Maggie Zebracka for always believing in me and this book. You never let me give up.

Most importantly, thank you to my mother, Ginger Renner. None of this would be possible without your continued support.

New and Forthcoming Releases

Blue Mistaken for Sky by Andrea Hollander

Thank Your Lucky Stars by Sherrie Flick

Luxury, Blue Lace by S. Brook Corfman ◆ Winner of the 2018 Rising Writer Prize, selected by Richard Siken

Anxious Attachments by Beth Alvarado

The Last Visit by Chad Abushanab ◆ Winner of the 2018 Donald Justice Poetry Prize, selected by Jericho Brown

Cage of Lit Glass by Charles Kell ◆ Winner of the 2018 Autumn House Poetry Prize, selected by Kimiko Hahn

Not Dead Yet and Other Stories by Hadley Moore ◆ Winner of the 2018 Autumn House Fiction Prize, selected by Dana Johnson

Limited by Body Habitus: An American Fat Story by Jennifer Renee Blevins ◆ Winner of the 2018 Autumn House Nonfiction Prize, selected by Daisy Hernández

Belief Is Its Own Kind of Truth, Maybe by Lori Jakiela

For our full catalog please visit: autumnhouse.org

Chad Abushanab is a poet, teacher, and critic. His poems have appeared in *The Believer*, *32 Poems*, *Southern Poetry Review*, *Ecotone*, *The Hopkins Review*, *The Southeast Review*, *Shenandoah*, *Best New Poets 2017*, and several other journals and anthologies. He holds an MFA from Vanderbilt University and a PhD in Literature and Creative Writing from Texas Tech University. Originally from South Carolina, he currently resides in Iowa City.